THE PLANETS

in Full Score

Gustav Holst

DOVER PUBLICATIONS, INC.
Mineola, New York

Bibliographical Note

This Dover edition, first published in 1996, is an unabridged republication of the music originally published by Goodwin & Tabb Ltd., London, 1921, in an edition limited to 200 copies. The Dover edition adds lists of contents and instrumentation.
We are grateful to the Sibley Music Library, Eastman School of Music, for the loan of the score.

International Standard Book Number: 0-486-29277-0

Manufactured in the United States of America
Dover Publications, Inc., 31 East 2nd Street, Mineola, N.Y. 11501

Contents

THE PLANETS
Op. 32 (1914–16)

Instrumentation

4 Flutes [Fl.]
   Fl. III doubles Piccolo I [Picc.]
   Fl. IV doubles Piccolo II and Bass Flute in G [Bass Fl.]

3 Oboes [Ob.]
   Ob. III doubles Bass Oboe [B. Oboe]

English Horn [E. H.]
3 Clarinets in A, B♭ [Cl.]
Bass Clarinet in B♭ [Bcl.]
3 Bassoons [Bn.]
Double Bassoon [Dbn.]

6 Horns in F [Hrn.]
4 Trumpets in C [Trp.]
3 Trombones [Trb.]
Tenor Tuba in B♭ [Ten. Tub.]
Bass Tuba [Bass Tub.]

6 Timpani (*2 players*) [Timp.]

Percussion (*3 players*):
   Triangle [Tri.]
   Side Drum [S.D.]
   Tambourine
   Cymbals [Cymb.]
   Bass Drum [B.D.]
   Gong
   Bells
   Glockenspiel [Gl.]

Celesta [Cel.]
Xylophone   } (*2 players*)

2 Harps [Hp.]
Organ [Org.]

Double Chorus of Female Voices (SSA/SSA)*

1st, 2nd Violins [Vns.]
Violas [Vas.]
Cellos [Violoncello, Vc.]
Basses [Doublebasses, Db.]

*A wordless "Hidden Choir of female voices in 6 parts" sings in "Neptune"
(see performance note, p. 162), but nowhere does this or later editions of the
score specify how the pitches are to be vocalized.

I. MARS, the Bringer of War

Picc.
Fl.
Ob.
E.H.
Bass Ob.
Cl.
Bcl.
Bn.
Dbn.
Hrn.
I
II
Trp.
Ten. Trb.
Bass Trb.
Ten. Tub.
Bass Tub.
Timp.
Vns.
Vas.
Vc.
Db.

XII Rall. al Fine.
Picc.
Fl.
Ob.
E.H.
Bass Ob.
a 3
Cl.
Bcl.
Bn.
Dbn.
Hrn.
Trp.
Ten. Trb.
Bass Trb.
Ten. Tub.
Bass Tub.
Timp.
Gong
Vns.
Vas.
Vc.
Db.
ffff
XII Rall. al Fine.

II. Venus, the Bringer of Peace

III. MERCURY, the Winged Messenger

III. Mercury 57

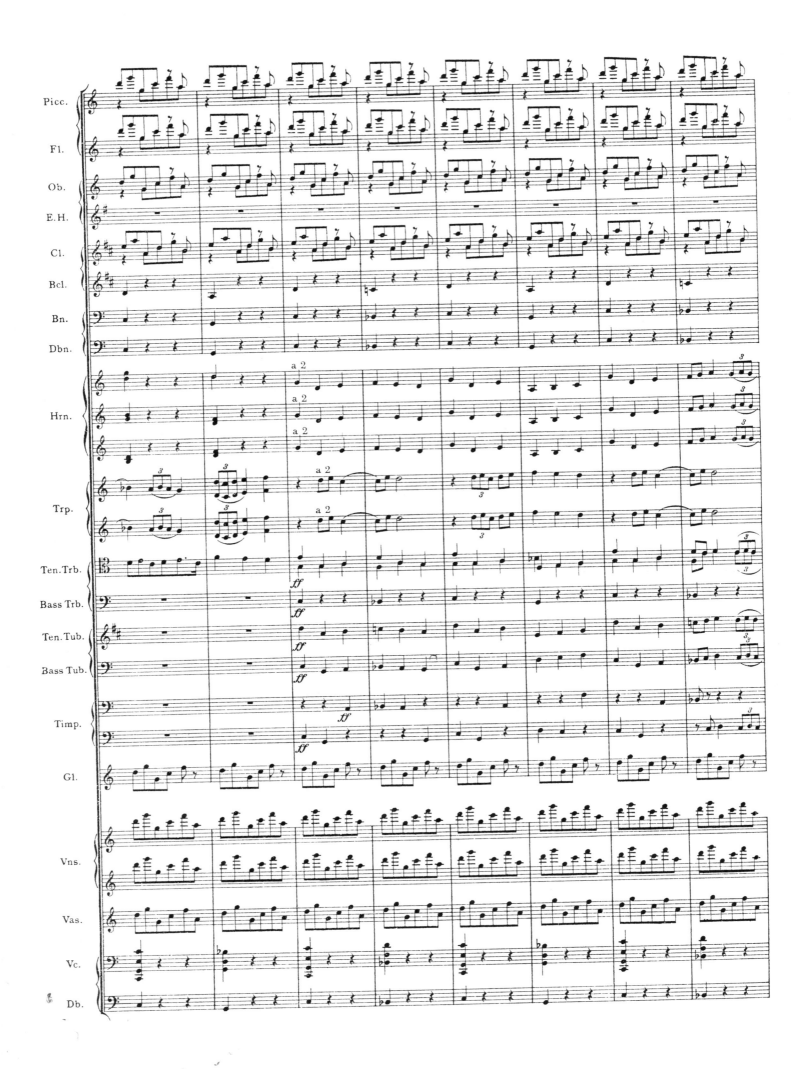

V. SATURN, the Bringer of Old Age

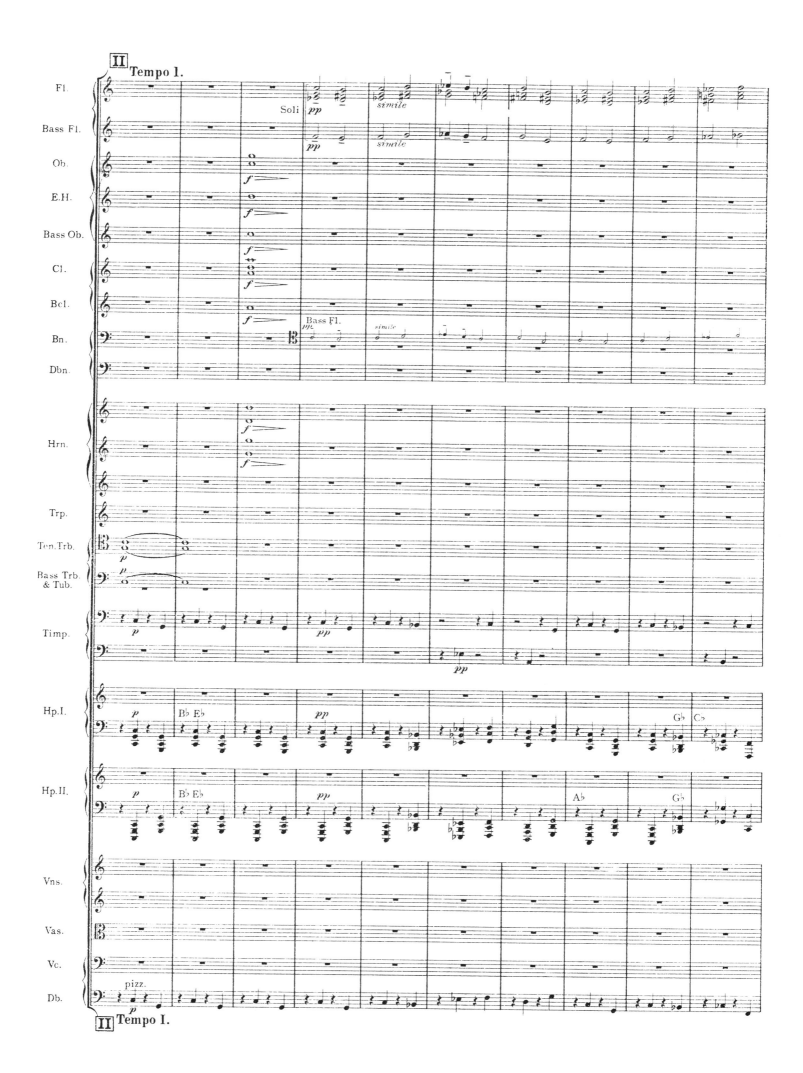

In the absence of Bass Flute 1st Clar. will play the small notes.

VI. URANUS, the Magician

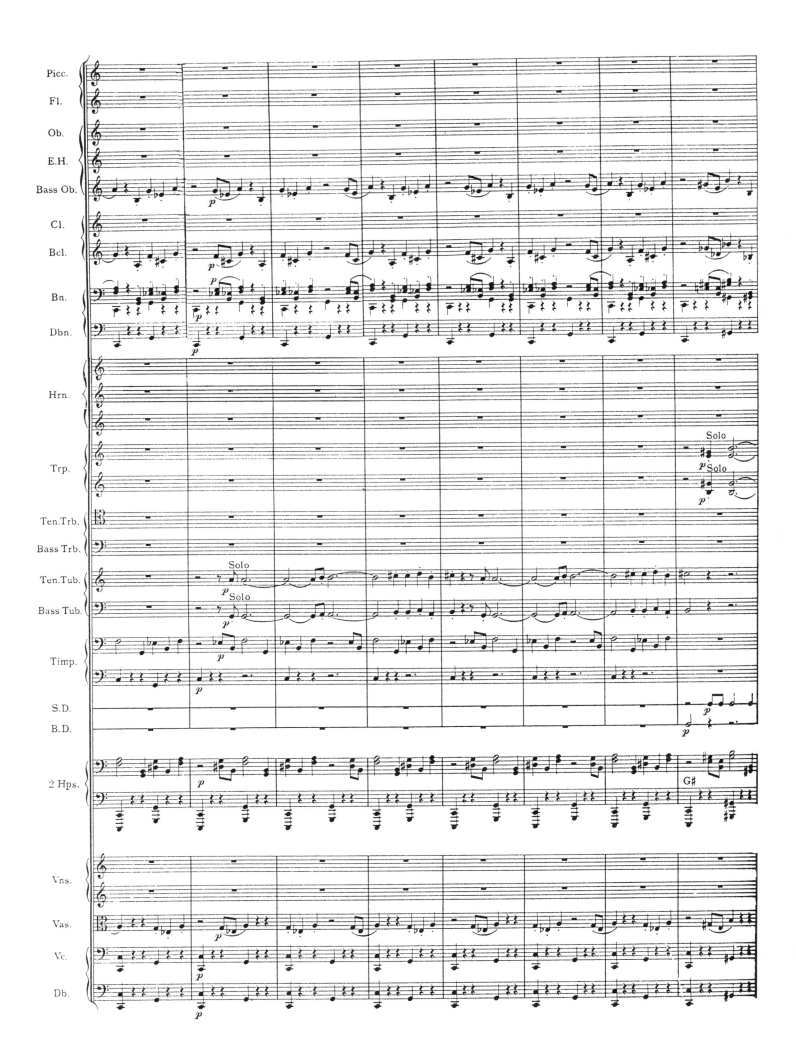

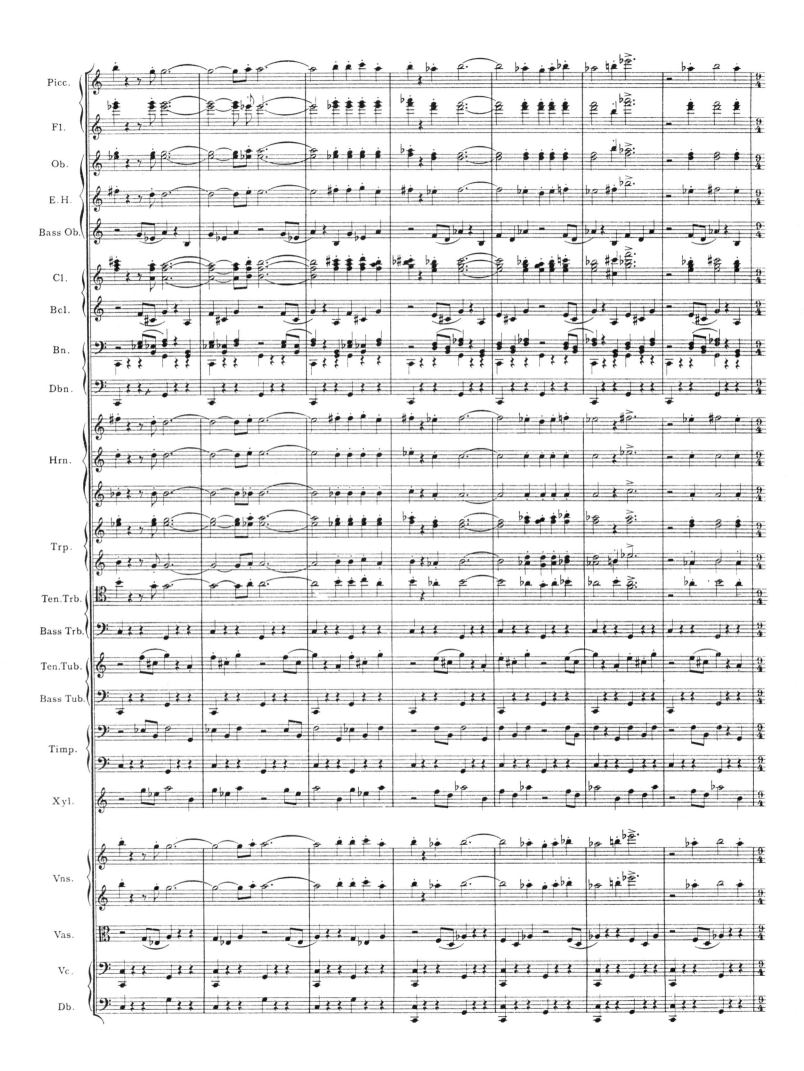

VII. Neptune, the Mystic

NB. The Orchestra is to play sempre *pp* throughout.

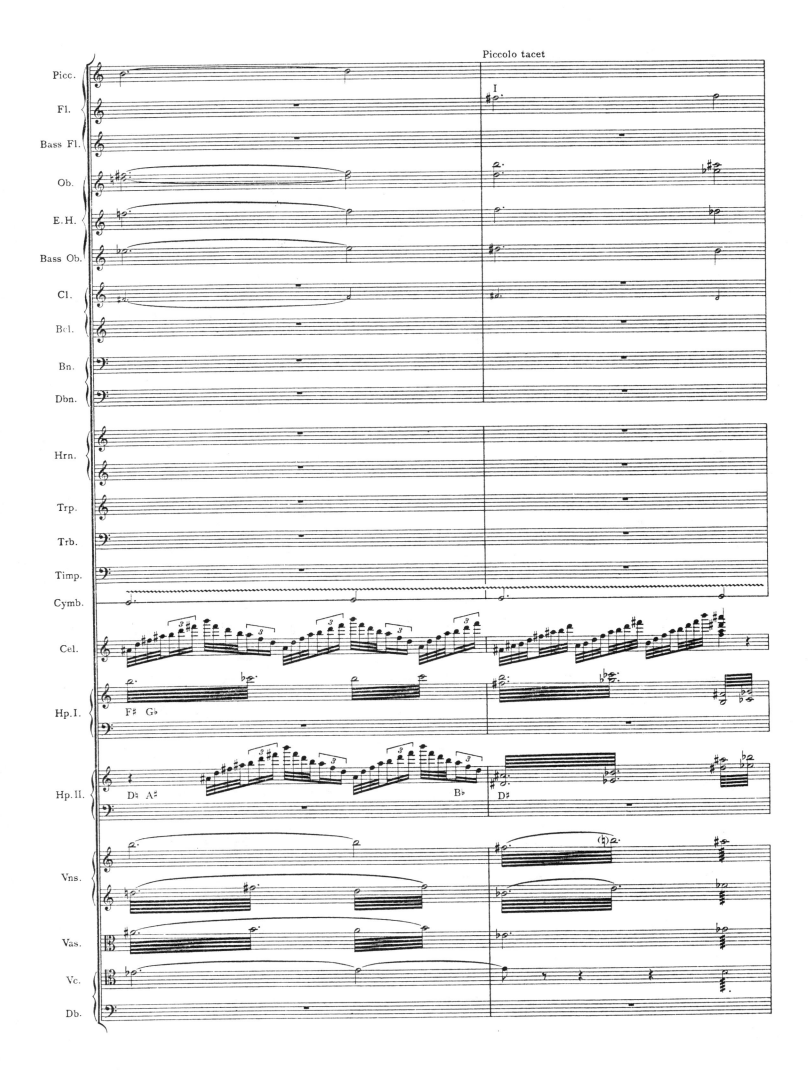

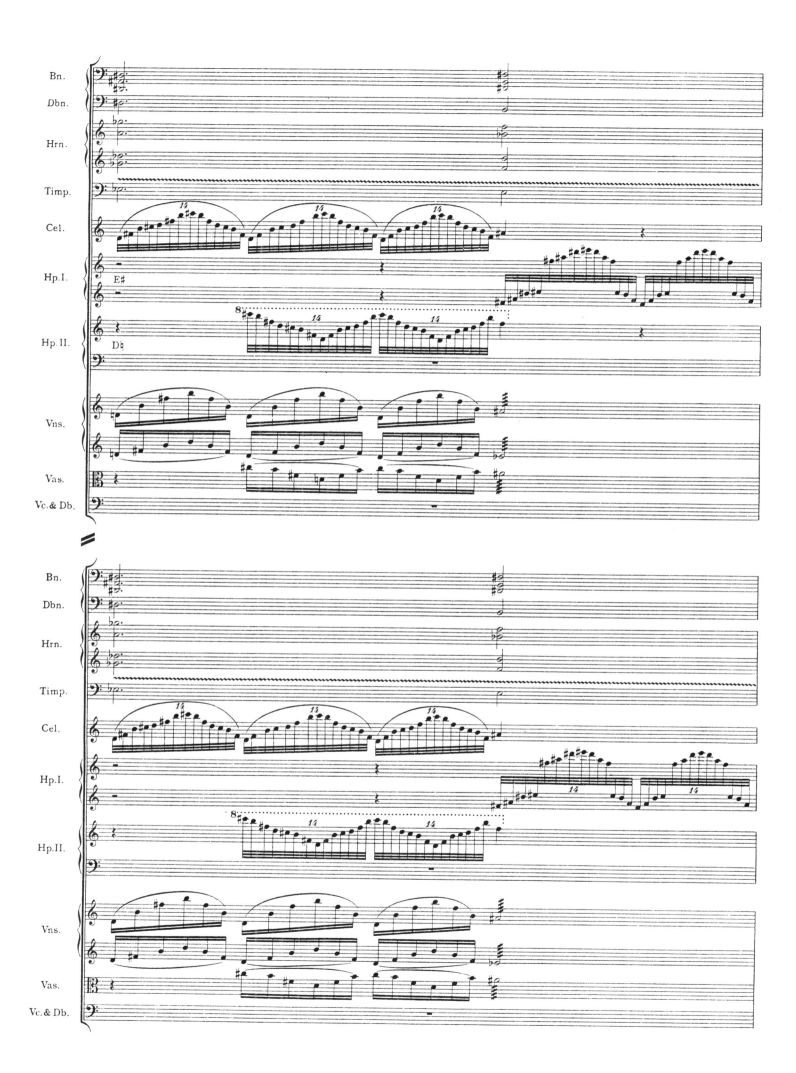

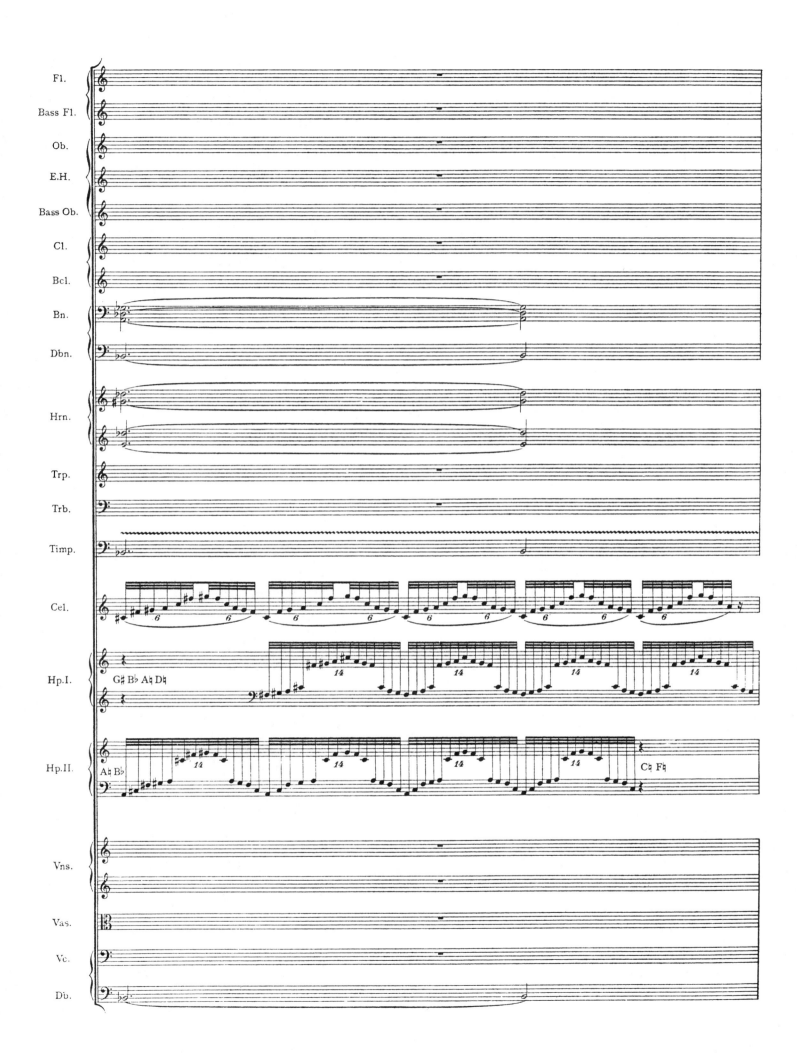

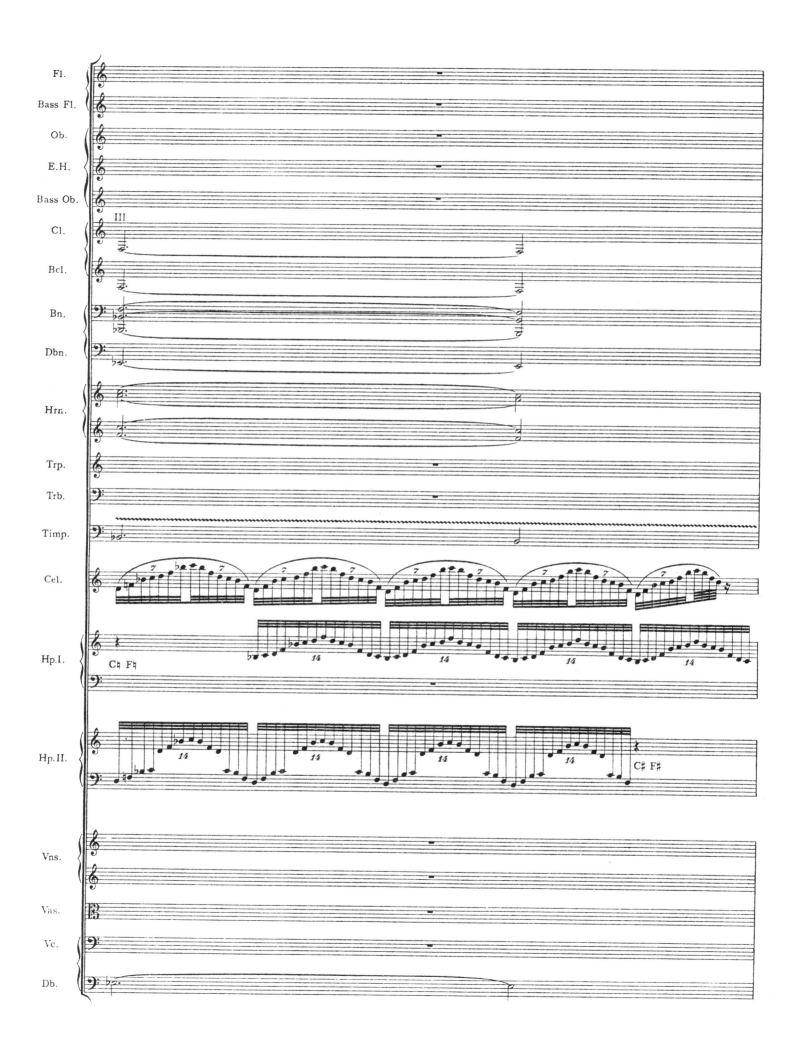

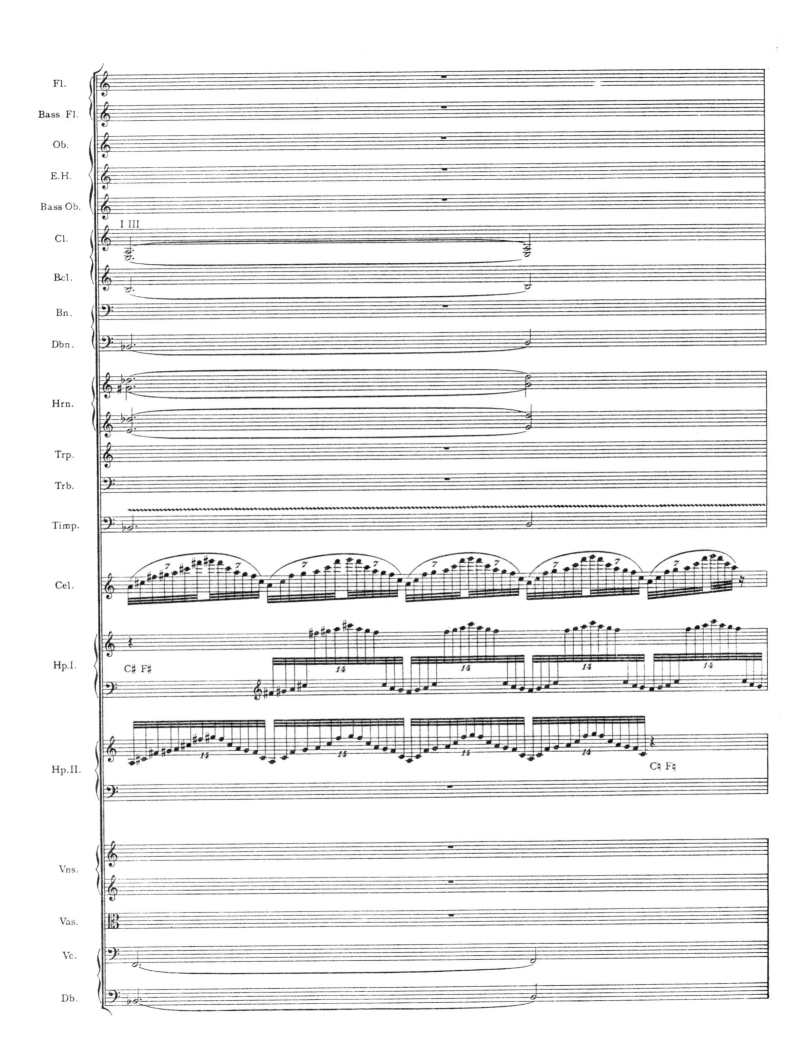

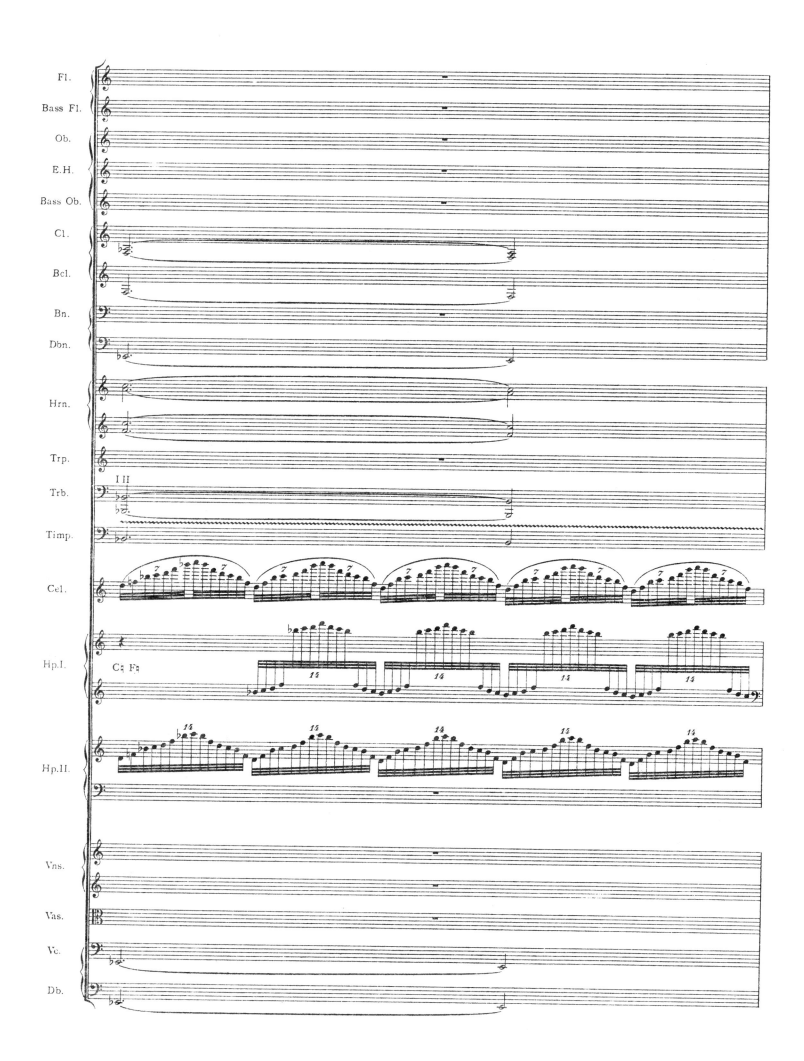

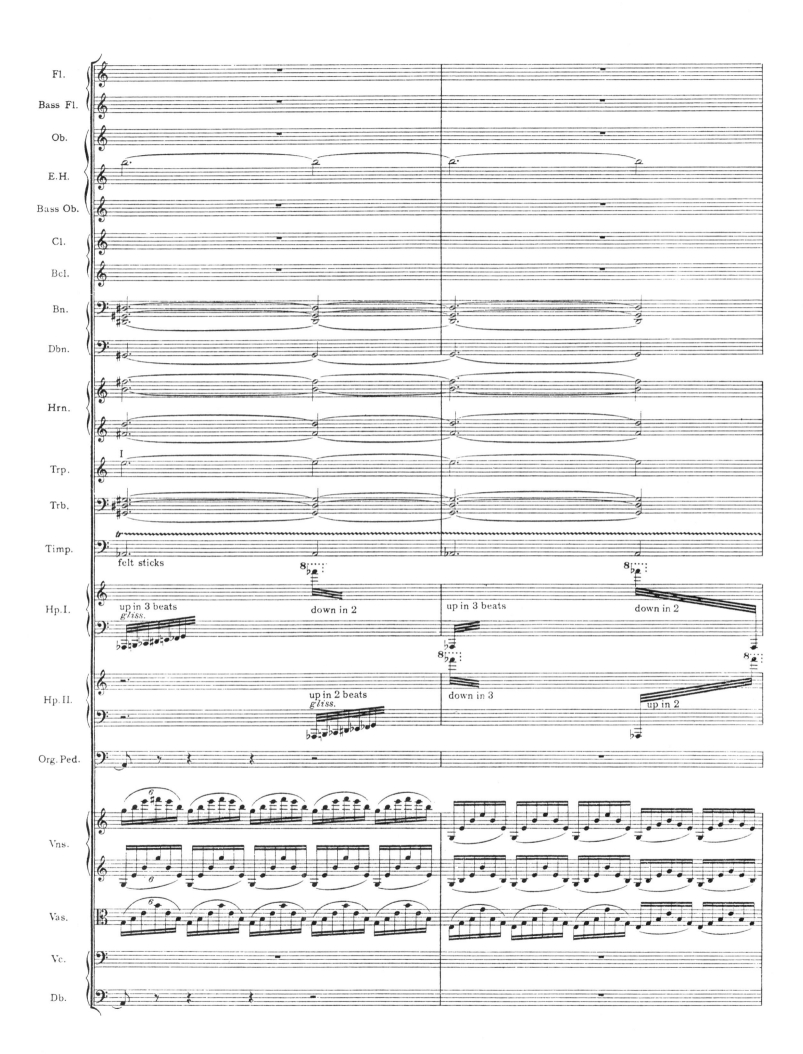

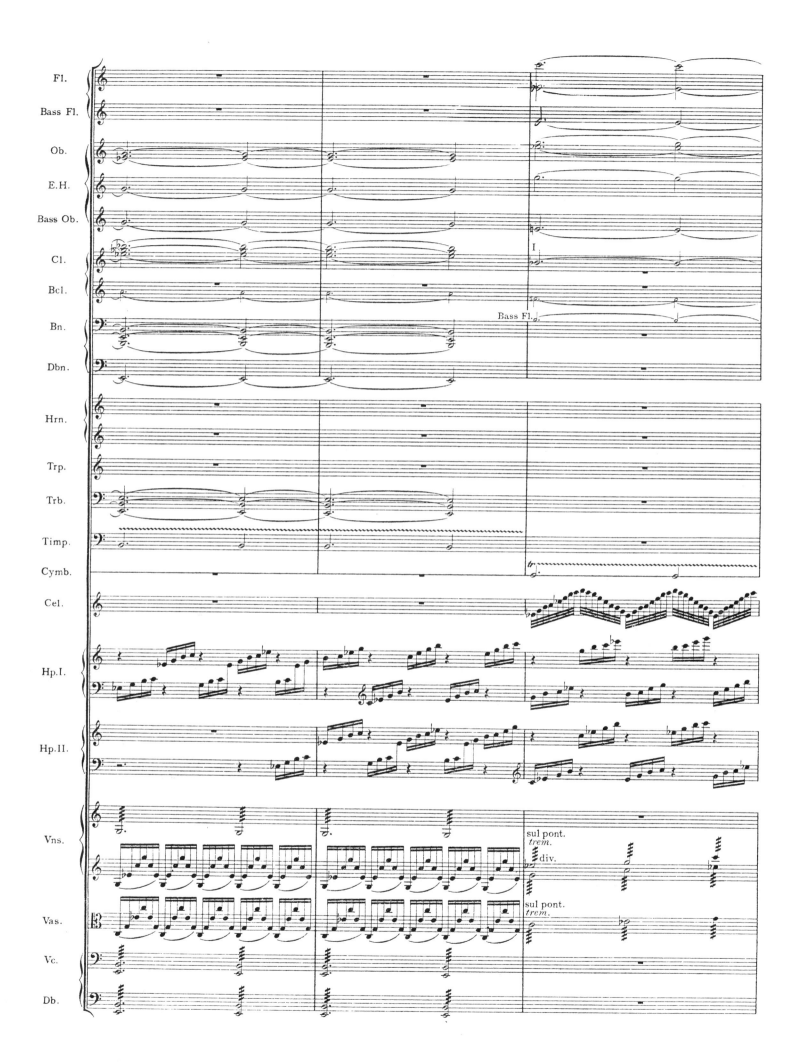

*) This bar to be repeated until the sound is lost in the distance.

END OF EDITION